These poems look with a steady eye, alert to enchantment and lost time, and to the human understanding and tende‑

—David Zieroth, author o

Terence Young awakens the extraord　　　　　　　　　　　　　m into "shining artifacts of memory"—to us　　　　　　　　　　　. Cohen. His mother's silver cigarette case, for example—his poems, like that cigarette case, can snap shut on the sadness and wonder of many things. Being a house-holder, a husband, a son, a father, and a grandfather, who sails far into these sensitive seas with his burden of loss, not bearing it like an albatross around his neck, but as a lantern of insight into conditions and concerns that are his, but common to us all. He is a master of that narrative edge in poetry and plain, but weighty language, which can carry those concerns, however light or heavy and follow every simple, but resonant detail till it cuts to the quick of a family crisis, quandary, or fondly recalled moment together with his son, his daughter, or his wife. It is not often we hear a poet tell so well the exhausting wonder of being a parent or who can look two ways at it, both as a son, and as a father. He peers just as perspicaciously both ways from the past into the present and the present into the past. Uncannily, it works like second sight. *Smithereens* is blessed with it.

　　　　—George McWhirter, joint winner of the Commonwealth
　　　　Poetry Prize for *Catalan Poems*

In his new collection *Smithereens* Terence Young's exquisite attention to detail collapses the distance between past and present bringing a startling immediacy to the work. Kaleidoscopic in nature, these poems transform the ordinary into the extraordinary. There is a deep affection at the heart of this book. With a back-ward glance, Young invokes a powerful history of the present.

　　　　—Eve Joseph, author of *Quarrels*

Terence Young's new collection is a valuable one: it is poetry you can fully trust. The respect for language, for experience—and the exemplary lacing together of the two across a rich range of emotion—are evident again and again in *Smithereens*. It is a collection to keep close at hand, a document of earned imagin-ative life, a fine lyrical record of how "what remains sings to us."

　　　　—Russell Thornton, author of *The Broken Face*

In Terence Young's long-awaited third book of poems, a four-year-old boy takes delight in blowing dandelion fluff to "smithereens," blissfully unaware that this is what time shall do to his life—and does to all our lives, even as they continue to unfold around us in the forward-moving inevitability of being lived. Young attempts less to reconstruct a life, or lives, well lived than to enact a kind of verbal psychometry. With a mental acuity that verges on the tactile, he carefully holds what evidence that remains—or as he puts it so aptly, the "alchemical symbols of / our confraternity / with impermanence"—in his mind and reads the resonances it gives off as best he can. Let me be the first to say that this poet's "best" is unerringly superlative. In these observant, at turns sardonic and tender poems about middle age (and, dare I say, slightly after), the fallout of how we humans tend to live is all around us. Young's remarkable achievement is to welcome such rich debris, sans the usual Proustian anguish, into our indebted present.

> —John Barton, author of *Lost Family*

The metaphors and deep feelings that jump out from behind everyday trees in *Smithereens* are like children who "hide in plain sight, crying surprise, surprise." Young's second book of poetry since his Governor General's Award nomination includes vivid and playful evocations of blowing dandelion seed, snapping a photo, a quince tree growing wild; small events enlivened by interiority, serious refection, and yes, surprise.

> —Cornelia Hoogland, author of *Cosmic Bowling*
> (with Ted Goodden)

From the young son's turn away from his father in "Blue Pontiac" to vultures rising from the brush in "Gathering," the poems in *Smithereens* are epiphanies on the move. Young's thinking process is an opening up of the close observation of an object, or a moment, into story, which is already a version of what was. The quotidian is everything even as it vanishes into memory.

> —Patrick Friesen, author of *Outlasting the Weather*

SMITHEREENS

Smithereens

poems

TERENCE YOUNG

HARBOUR
PUBLISHING

HARBOUR PUBLISHING CO. LTD.
P.O. Box 219, Madeira Park, BC, VON 2H0
www.harbourpublishing.com

Edited by Elaine Park
Cover design by Anna Comfort O'Keeffe
Text design by Shed Simas / Onça Design
Printed and bound in Canada
Printed on 100 percent recycled paper

Harbour Publishing acknowledges the support of the Canada
Council for the Arts, the Government of Canada, and the Province
of British Columbia through the BC Arts Council.

LIBRARY AND ARCHIVES CANADA CATALOGUING IN PUBLICATION
Title: Smithereens / Terence Young.
Names: Young, Terence, 1953– author.
Description: Poems.
Identifiers: Canadiana (print) 20200374753 | Canadiana
    (ebook) 20200374818 | ISBN 9781550179439 (softcover) |
    ISBN 9781550179446 (EPUB)
Classification: LCC PS8597.072 S65 2021 | DDC C811/.54—dc23

for Patricia, as always

CONTENTS

TENDER IS THE NIGHT

Tender Is the Night 3
Snowfall 5
Mixed Blessing 8
My Mother's Cigarette Case 10
The Bear 13
Urban Night Music 15
Tent Island Anchorage, 1962 17
Reunion 18
Just Married 20
Elegy 23
Easter Train 24
Food: A Fairy Tale 26
Daysailing During an Eclipse 28
Weight 30
Offertory 32

LEGACY

Legacy 37
The Morning Mike Dies 39
Look at the Time 41
The Latest Trends 43
The Animals Lie Down to Die 45
Infection 47
Blue Pontiac 49
Forgetting to Remember 51
Observations 53
Gathering 54
Metaphysics on the Cheap 56
Matins 58
Absolution 60

Surcease   62

Four Erasures   63

From the Land of Sky-Blue Waters   65

Fern Island Candle®   66

Gary   67

Weather News   69

PRANAYAMA

Pranayama   73

On Aging   74

Shelf Life   76

The Rites of Spring   77

The Things They've Ruined   80

Volunteers   82

Younger Than That Now   84

On First Viewing the Extent of the Beaver Invasion   86

Stat Holiday   88

The Uncertainty Principle   90

Travelogue   91

The Party   92

Against Awe   95

EPILOGUE

What We Keep   99

What We Save For Last   101

What Remains   102

ACKNOWLEDGEMENTS   104

ABOUT THE AUTHOR   104

TENDER IS THE NIGHT

TENDER IS THE NIGHT

Halfway through the voyage, while I sleep below decks,
the ferry turns around for some medical emergency,

so that when I wake, a little hungry, and venture upstairs
for coffee, a muffin, I look outside to find our ship arriving

at a harbour I don't recognize, lit up by the setting sun, a
golden port out of the *Odyssey*—houses I've never seen

before, boats at anchor that look vaguely European, at least
for the lovely five minutes my bearings are shattered, and I am

imagining a new life, enchanted—I hope literally—about
to disembark on a foreign shore, perhaps in a parallel universe,

where every street is unknown, feeling a little like stout Cortez
in Keats's poem, when he first sees the Pacific:

> Silent, upon a peak in Darien

though not as grand or literary, more like a kid who can't believe
his room contains a real secret passageway, almost blinking and

rubbing my eyes to see if the mirage will disappear, which it does,
immediately, when the woman next to me complains how late

she'll be now, thanks to this about-face, the early sailing not such
a good idea after all in hindsight, unaware she has broken the most

vivid waking dream of my life and left me as disappointed as Keats
must have been when some pedant pointed out it was Balboa, not

Cortés, who first set European eyes westward from that mountain
top, a name that so spoiled the meter of his line he refused to change

it, certain till his death that facts had little to do with truth or beauty.

SNOWFALL

They've been sounding out
the names of the dead: friends,
relatives, this year's crop of
writers, musicians,

something to do while
they are driving the long road
between the last town
and the next.

So many now,
and those they forget
hang between them
like the empty spaces
in a crossword.

Their route takes them
high into snow country,
where flurries descend and
silence the game,
wet, heavy flakes that ·
slow the car's wipers,
narrow the view.

Used to be
they'd tell themselves
the departed were old,
but they're old now too,
so they no longer mention
anyone's age.

The few who died young
remain bright, as though the sun
had been shining at the time,
but they both know
it is only their own youth
that glows.

When the roster ends,
they speculate on whose name
may next pass their lips,
but briefly, because to do so
feels reckless.

Better to marvel
at the list itself,
how long it has grown,
how death has worn thin,
as if to be alive
were the true miracle.

Their hotel that night is
The Village Green,
which they booked hoping
for a peaceful place,
where townspeople might gather
to talk with friends and
forget their hard lives,

but it is nothing like that,
only a white box
in a parking lot of white,
and they spend the evening
watching TV shows from the past,
laughing again at all the actors
they haven't seen for years.

MIXED BLESSING

For a while we called it the good fire,
the best fire, the fire that saved us

because we were insured, and the insurance
paid for all the things we could never afford,

the new wiring and plumbing and paint
and sofas and stereos and computers

and clothes and pots and pans and bicycles
and carpets and curtains and state-of-the-art

smoke detectors for the next fire, but
every once in a while, an image of our

old basement kitchen will shove its way
to the front row of my thought parade

and I will believe, as I do sometimes in dreams
about things I've lost to disease, the years, the

insatiable ocean, that it still exists somewhere,
behind a door that I have only to open

and walk through to find our son, seated at
the makeshift bar, eating a snack after school,

my wife down on her knees trying to clean
the hopelessly stained lino, our daughter

about to arrive with her boyfriend, and me too,
fiddling with the coffee maker that started

the whole conflagration in the first place,
only this time deciding not to repair it, un-

plugging the thing instead and carrying it wisely
to my workshop where all toys and appliances

went to die, and leaving it there, returning
with a bottle of terrible homemade wine

which I pour into a couple of glasses from
the cupboard where we used to store our

hippy goblets made from clay and the poisonous
lead decanters handed down, the sorts of things

we never replaced after they burned, like the
Victrola and my father's pewter mug, or couldn't,

like our youngest's kindergarten rendering of a
tugboat—blue hull, aquamarine ocean, blowing

billows of smoke into a cloudless and benign sky.

MY MOTHER'S CIGARETTE CASE

I still have it somewhere,
her initials engraved, all three,
C.A.Y. in curling capitals, the surface
tarnished because who polishes
silver anymore?

I've seen a dozen similar
at Value Village,
tossed out by children who are better
at letting go,
so few interested in relics
from an age that is still
too recent.

It flips opens like an old-school
cellphone, two neat halves that part,
the cigarettes all in a row,
tilting up.

I used it for a while
to hold my own,
an affectation I liked,
the formality,
how I would draw it
from an inner jacket pocket,
select one
as though I were choosing
a diamond from a display case.

But cigarettes became so long
I'd have to cut them to fit, and
I hadn't the patience,
dropped it in a drawer,
then into a box that might be
in the attic.

On evenings they had guests,
my father in grey, my mother in
green silk,
I'd watch her reach for it
in her purse
or lift it from the coffee table,
the way she'd light up
and breathe in,
allowing some smoke
to remain hanging, which
she'd take in a second later
through her nose,
French inhaling it was called,
a name that made her
even more attractive.

She would hold it
flat against her palm
until an errand claimed her,
then set it aside discreetly.

Once, I picked it up, still warm
from her grip, a bright, lovely thing
that made me want it
the way I want it even now,
years after I have given up
the habit,
if only for the sound it made
when she snapped it shut.

THE BEAR

Woken from an afternoon nap, you rise only to descend your wood-
butcher stairway, past the vaulted, multi-mullioned window on whose

other side now sits a bear, Buddha-like, on his backside, head concealed
in the Rubbermaid garbage can he holds aloft between two paws.

In sixty summers, you've never seen such a creature anywhere near
this place, found no scat, heard no tales of neighbours' fruit trees

bent or broken, undaunted for all this time to ramble, kids in tow,
down the remnant logging roads and deer paths that make a park

of these toy woods, so close to town now town has devoured all the
land between. Yet here he sits, or she, for all you know, fur so black

it's almost blue, only thin glass between you, so suddenly proximate
you are pressed to say what you are seeing, this vaudeville act, ursine

slapstick Chaplin who invites you to forget all danger, to forget you
are still one animal coming upon another. A single noisy tread, one

telltale stair, and you are busted, as the beautiful comedian detects
your gaze behind the fifteen panes that transform bear to cubist

caricature, your clown of darkness, who regains all fours and turns
literal tail to amble, not run, back into the maze of forest and con-

spiratorial salal, but not before you throw sense and caution to the
wind, wrench open the back door and follow at a distance, axe in

hand, berating your bruin-buffoon for transforming forever this be-
nign acreage into something less safe, if more magical, where visiting

spirits leave behind their perfect signature, which, to all who will
listen over dinner and wine, you reveal with a flourish at the tale's

end, the garbage can's rectangular lid and four neat punctures,
arranged in a fan, an arc, like a winning hand of poker, jokers wild.

URBAN NIGHT MUSIC

Mostly percussion
few lyrics
anti-melodies of
discordant timpani
hollow metal dumpsters
their lids opening
and slamming shut
the mingled vitreous chime
of empty litres and
half-litres falling into
rolling carts of
chrome and plastic
from whose hardened wheels
an intermittent drone
runs the length
of this alley
outside our window
as on a staff, bass and
treble notes competing
staccato outbursts
solos and duets
car alarm grace notes
and soprano sirens
rising and fading
crescendo and
decrescendo
while the low rumble of
buses two streets away
augments the cascade
of water falling
through gutter pipes
a susurrus of rain
escaping back to

the sea
soaking the musicians
themselves
who sleep out in it
the original unpaid buskers
on street corners
under bridges
singing their legato lives
one note at a time.

TENT ISLAND ANCHORAGE, 1962

Salt air leaks in
through canvas that is
dew-damp this August morning,
our dying sun drying
pilot-house, foredeck, saloon
top to bottom as it rises
behind sandstone bluffs.

My parents, sister, still sleep,
dream through the insouciant dawn,
deaf to the voice of water
that against our hull
protests its displacement.

Before long, the scent
of late summer maple, then
arbutus bark, broom and fir needles,
a riot in our cockpit shroud,
last night's beach fire too.

REUNION

They are old friends, all of them,
together again around the oak table

with its clever drop leaves, the table
itself going back to their youth, their

teenage years and afterwards, when
they first got jobs, fell in love, married,

had children, all those so-called mile-
stones, together again, this time for

a healthy lunch, some red wine, a meet-
ing to measure change—who has let

her hair go grey, who has not—to share
photographs of nieces, nephews, grand-

sons, granddaughters, but mostly to raise
a glass to a woman of ninety-three who

knew them during those early days, the
mother of a boyfriend one of the women

had for a while, then didn't, like a lot of
boyfriends who came and went, leaving

them his mother, who refused to go any-
where, endearing herself until she was

as much family as if the boyfriend had never
left, which he hasn't, still popping in now

and then to say hello, charming them all
over again, or trying to, before returning

to his distant life in a mythical country,
older now himself, hair thinning, altered,

as each of these women is, by worry, by
loss, by time, like all of them a survivor,

who has become dear the way we all do
if we live long enough, simply for surviving,

like his determined parent, who is also
sitting at this venerable table, happy

to have a glass of merlot in front of her,
some salad and fresh chard to take home,

and another chance to tell the story of
her father, how he and she once swam

at a beach not far from here, while her
mother gathered driftwood, lit a fire

under a blackened kettle for their tea.

JUST MARRIED

A motel on an island,
a cabin above a bay.
The tap water smells,
towels refuse to dry.

They walk trails,
eat dinners of ham
with pineapple and rice,
play table tennis.

Their car is a joke.
Their suitcases belong
to their parents.

She sleeps badly.
He can't wake up.

An older couple
befriends them on a beach.
There is talk of mutual funds,
of long-term savings.

In a community hall,
they dance to music
they once made fun of.

They rise late,
stare at each other's
arms, shoulders, backs,
long legs,

imagine how many years
will have to pass before
they take what they see
for granted,

how such a day
might ever arrive,

promise never
to forget a minute,
though even now
they are forgetting.

They talk, and
what they talk about
sinks beyond recall.

The times
they make love
disappear until
they make love again.

They are losing them-
selves even as they find
each other, like
Hansel and Gretel

whose way home
is consumed crumb by
crumb while they move
deeper and deeper
into darkness.

If they had a camera,
they would take pictures,
but pictures record
only what was,

what they cannot
have again, so it is
better they don't,
better they keep

walking into a
future unburdened
by this love that will
leave them

as stars leave
each morning, slowly,
imperceptibly, as though
they'd never been there
at all.

ELEGY

Making love
in September once
the leaves fallen
the world all around them falling
when they were young
and didn't believe
they were falling too.

They were falling too
and didn't believe
when they were young
the world all around them falling
the leaves fallen
in September once
making love.

EASTER TRAIN

The bunny's on a coffee break or late lunch, but clearly absent
for unlucky us, who have walked here from Vancouver's storied

West End in hopes of an audience and a ride through the temperate
rainforest of Stanley Park, our daughter's suggestion to distract this

four-year-old boy temporarily in our care, while she and his father
try to recreate one of those afternoons and evenings they used to

take for granted. Each miniature railcar is a study in scale, an exer-
cise in memory, what it once was like to be small, to not have to

hunch, the same revelation I had visiting my own children's primary
school years ago, noting the height of the water fountains, the

lowered urinals in the boys' washroom, those ridiculous desks
parents sat in during interviews, whatever dignity they might own

negated by their diminished stature, a lesson in what it means to
be a child. We roll through tunnels where orange and purple mush-

rooms glow, lit, presumably, by hidden LEDs and eerily reminiscent
of Alice, who also has nothing to do with this season of Christ's

crucifixion, but essential nonetheless, if only because a black tunnel
is a scary thing, too stark a metaphor for another kind of darkness

and our dopey hope of light at the other end. The goal is to spot
the eggs, a task that is not a task, since they are everywhere, gold

and green, large and small, piled under giant ferns, on top of
antique farm equipment, next to Indigenous carvings of ravens

and eagles, a contrast that offers an instant course in post-colonial
studies, as well as a hint that this train is the plotline of several

narratives, Christmas being the biggest hit, or so I'm told. When
we disembark, the bunny has reappeared, holding court and glad-

handing with his adoring public, high-fiving the pint-sized fans
who reach out to touch their idol, a train-ride too late for our dis-

enchanted grandson, who, once snubbed, is unforgiving, ready
to move along and forego any photo-op in favour of the jelly-

bean hunt, where he hopes to clean up, as he did on the way
here when we stopped at a boulevard full of dandelions, happy

to take his sweet time blowing to smithereens each and every one.

FOOD: A FAIRY TALE

The parents grew the usual things in their backyard—not a victory
garden because this was after the war—mostly carrots and peas, which

the children they'd always dreamed of having liked very much, and
chard and spinach, which the children hated, and reams of raspberries

which the mother boiled into jars of jam for the winter, along with
pears for dessert and applesauce made from the Kings on their tree,

filling the preserve cupboard in the basement, until one day
the parents stopped gardening and sowed the beds with easy grass

and bought food from the new supermarket, which the children liked
equally well, or even better, and the years passed and the children

grew into hippies and took a stab at growing their own lettuce and
tomatoes in the middle of forests where the soil was piss poor

and so deficient in nutrients that the lettuce shot up broad and
pale green and the tomatoes bore no fruit at all, and the children

gave up and moved into the city, where they had their own children
who grew up far too quickly and turned their backs on dairy and meat

and eggs and forced their parents to shun all processed food and to
tear up the lawn for potatoes and broccoli and kale and onions and

beans and beets, advising them on appropriate methods of pruning and
fertilizing and rotation, so that in the end their aging parents found

something about their lives they had forgotten and got their hands
dirty with manure and compost, instead, and sat at the dining room

table with their children and grandchildren, filling their faces with salad after salad and teriyaki beans and roasted fennel root, raising their

glasses of homemade beer and toasting their labours, the wisdom of the young, and the boundless patience of the good earth.

DAYSAILING DURING AN ECLIPSE

The city's harbour
in half-light,
some angel child
twisting a cosmic
dimmer switch,

everything Turner-
esque, all watery glass,
angled hulls and masts,
buildings clad in
smoky translucence,
a late Romantic post-
apocalyptic haze

we move through
convinced of our own
significance, past
doomed kayakers and
warning beacons
that urge us to
turn back,
abandon any
hope we entertain
of dropping anchor
in a safe bay,
of finishing our
sandwiches and tea,

while all around us,
on deck and
canvas, on sidewalks
and streets throughout
town, heaven carves
scallops of shade,
crescent fingerprints
of partial sun-death
that earth and asphalt
wear like tattoos,

alchemical symbols of
our confraternity
with impermanence,
everyone momentarily
branded where they stand,
prisoners of an
epiphany that lasts
only minutes,

more than enough time
to snap a photo and
send it across
continents and oceans
as proof of miracles,
our perilous lives.

WEIGHT

Let us recall people we have carried
on our backs, like the girl this boy is hefting

to prove he can, outside our local at closing,
on a mid-November night thick with rain,

both of them astonished by arms, thighs,
to be so alive beneath their winter coats.

Or the waitress I carried one December,
across a snowy field in Thompson, Manitoba,

sometime cook, too, in a coffee shop,
generous with her portions of pancakes and

eggs, lonely in a town of lonely people,
out on her break that Christmas day, walking

under the frozen Northern sun in parka,
thin shoes, me in boots and useless jeans,

the snow deep enough to invite such
a game, wondering as I did with almost

every sympathetic face back then, was
this someone to love, that whole mystery.

But to get back to those kids outside the
pub, as my wife and I walk by, the boy,

his knees locked against buckling, the girl
turning her head to smile at a cellphone,

its flash lighting up the street, his face
and behind him hers, stunned, joyous,

bright echo of the photo someone took
of the waitress, nameless now, and me,

black and white study in self-consciousness,
our two shadows crisp against the snow.

OFFERTORY

In an aerogram
      to my mother in 1943,
            my father recalls the day

they watched
      King George VI
            roll by the family home

during a state visit
      in May, before the war,
            before their marriage,

not to marvel
      or reminisce,
            but to ask whether

she remembers
      what they talked about
            later that same afternoon,

seated before the
      great front window
            overlooking the street,

if the question
      embarrasses her,
            if to choose the names

of children
      they may one day have
            is also to speak of sex,

which at the time
      was a delicate subject,
            though understandably of interest

to a young man
      hunkered down
            in a battle he probably believed

he would not survive,
      but did, along with
            my name and my sister's,

which he and
      my mother wielded
            like talismans, entertaining

no alternatives,
      steadfast in their choices
            for another decade, as though

they had entered
      into some kind of pact,
            not to honour their former selves,

nor to carry
      a small part of their
            earlier delight with each other

into the future, but
      to thank the fickle god
            who had allowed them to live.

LEGACY

LEGACY

Male mountain lions will kill their young
male polar bears too.
No wonder these kits and cubs
head for high ground as soon
as their legs will carry them.

As soon as their legs will carry them
they head for high ground
the way we might if our fathers
hunted us down, their faces
appearing out of nowhere
in our dreams.

In our dreams, our fathers' faces
appear out of nowhere
long after they have gone
long after we have fled
to start a new life in the wake
of their fierce and quiet love.

In the wake of their fierce and
quiet love, we start our new lives
on ships and islands and distant continents
where we slip into the dreams
of our own sons, who mistake
silence for something else.

Our sons mistake silence
for something else
that we cannot explain
not to them or their mothers
except to say it is our inheritance
a gift handed down
a wind that keeps us moving.

There is a wind that keeps us moving
as soon as our legs will carry us
a fierce and quiet love
that appears in our dreams
in the dreams of our sons too
long after our fathers have gone.

THE MORNING MIKE DIES

—remembering Mike Matthews (1937–2012)

The morning Mike dies, I fix the printer, find some cookies
I like at the market, even snag a free six-pack from the liquor store

because the clerk's scanner fouls up—leave before she figures
it out, before I do too. "Good stuff," Mike would've said, words

everyone says, just not the way he did, as though a treasure chest
had opened, rubbing his hands together, eyes agoggle. Always

thought he'd grow old, older than seventy-four, which sounds old
but wasn't when Mike turned it, a big man even then who made

everyone else feel bigger. In the car, I wonder aloud if I should take
back the beer, how much time will pass before inventory catches

up with my small theft. What Mike would've done I can only guess.
After the email, I open a pilsner for my wife, an extra-special bitter

for me, and we raise our glasses to Mike. A most beautiful song
is playing, one we've never heard, just when we are thinking we've

heard everything. Out the window more of the lake's ice has retreated,
the liberated water once again a mirror for the orange tint on the clouds,

the bright blue between. "Come look," I say. I think of Mike's arms and
legs and broad shoulders, his eyes, those feet that carried him through

the marathon of years, and then try not to think of them, as I do with
anything I have lost forever. Mike would return the beer, if only to

show the clerk her gadget was faulty, that she'd be better off with a
pad and pencil, her God-given brain, than to have faith in a machine,

which Mike would never do, happiest the way I remember him, with a
stovetop espresso, cast-iron frying pan, a decent blade to chop the garlic.

LOOK AT THE TIME

Hydro's high-rigger checks his gear once, twice,
before topping our right-of-way's lifeless grand fir,

chainsaw swinging from his hip, orange helmet
dripping rain. Ten-foot lengths fall, plant them-

selves deep in forest bracken, each bucked section
landing heavier than the last until what's left poses

no danger to power lines. When he leaves, I count
rings, watch years come and go by quarter-inches,

stop when I reach my age. Every winter of my life,
each spring, contour lines on a map—childhood,

adolescence, marriage—all here, charted and con-
tained in this dismembered trunk, which I will burn

piece by piece, releasing energy stored before I could
even speak. If only I could burrow between these layers,

drill into a single year, breathe that air again, see every-
one as they once were, walk down streets as though

they were new, recover all of that, gather it up, hold it
more firmly than I held it then, when days were for

squandering and nights passed in a blink. This balsam
grew until it could grow no longer, needles turning

brown, sap retreating, roots relinquishing their grasp,
alive only with bugs eating their way through Augusts

and Aprils, from drought to deluge, obliterating days
and weeks, whole decades with their hunger. Summer

heat will dry what I scavenge, wedges I will split and
split again, feeding them when October comes into

an iron maw that will transform history's sunshine
to flame and smoke, release it into the autumn air.

THE LATEST TRENDS

Leonard drones in amphibrachic tetrameter about
his famous blue raincoat, accompanied by a few

clicks and hisses, courtesy the aging vinyl that contains
his voice. To cue the song and drop the needle is an

anodyne for the painful ease of playlists selected by
algorithms on machines that profess to know our taste

in music, books, film, which they clearly do with an
accuracy that is both amazing and depressing, though

it really should come as no surprise that we are not
unique in our attraction to lugubrious songs about

anguished love triangles, because as any good algorithm
knows, the human species cut its teeth on self-inflicted

wounds, if only to have something to sing or write about.
No surprise to discover that those who bought *Love &*

Hate also bought *Rain Dogs*, who loved *L'Étranger*
also loved *Heart of Darkness*, who watched *Hiroshima*

mon amour also watched *The 400 Blows*. Only the hard-core
romantic insists it is better to stumble upon a novel, an album,

a work of art, that a title suggested during a brief encounter
at the market or on the bus is glorious serendipity and that

guidance is a word better reserved for the private realms of
religion, like divine will or karma, those older organizing

principles once said to know us and direct us the way iTunes
does now. The haphazard aisles of an independent bookstore,

songs heard in passing on the radio, liner notes—all "shining
artifacts of the past," as Leonard says, like window shopping

through real glass, or kneeling next to the turntable, its
simple arm, and filling our lungs to blow away the dust.

THE ANIMALS LIE DOWN TO DIE

A broad cedar's
lower branches fan wide
above a dry, soft vellum of
years of needles and
the skeleton of a deer,
undisturbed, a curled calligraphy
of vertebrae and delicate
femurs, skull and lower jaw,
a few cursive hairs.

It lies off the trail, hidden
from view in these illegible woods
unlogged for more than
a hundred years, springboard
cuts like graffiti from another age
still visible on stumps and
some of the mature firs
the fallers spared.

Hospice workers say
the dying take their cue
to go when vigilant friends
leave the room—a smoke,
a drink, a bite
to eat—as though the work
of death is a private business
that needs a person's full
attention, free of
attendant grief, the mourner's
urge to edit the page,
to redact.

The deer's instinct
told it to avoid the open field
a few hundred yards away,
to shun the noisy dialogue of cloud
and sun in favour of shade, of
the whispered hieroglyphics
of eternity.

My mother, too, composed
her departure in secret, while
her family read or slept, curled up
in hospital loungers nearby, a furtive exit
we registered only after
breath had left her, the indecipherable
moment of translation hers,
and hers alone.

INFECTION

I

My child's fever, his sharp pain,
the sudden pang as each tympanum

ruptures, a boy deafened, bleeding
from both ears, while I am thinking

emergency room, gas mask, oblivion.

II

Spring break he navigated moguls
pretended not to hear me yell, curse,

bid him slow down on the ski hill,
the sun bright as Bahrain's, and I

a cantankerous nuisance, improbable
as a brontosaurus, for the first time lost

in the open air I used to own, in grimy
jeans and thrift store snow boots, his

wordless dismissal a hydrogen bomb
meant to obliterate me, the fact of me,

all the years I'd spent with him,
an angry migrant in my custody,

eager for his papers, citizenship.

III

Out of his sick bed he is thin as air,
in my arms weightless as wheat, as

alliteration itself, and I am his saviour
in jacket and tie, descending the stairs,

feeling like Davy Crockett at my own
private Alamo, cursing all bacteria,

micro-hoodlums trying to rob me, nasty
as the cheeseburger I know he'll want,

his reward for being stoic, for submitting
to doctors and anaesthetists, for suffering

the comedy of his father who nearly drops
him on the boulevard next to our parked car,

where I set him on his mother's waiting lap,
she and I the smiling con artists who have led

this creature up the garden path with promises
of summer picnics at the lake, Christmas mornings,

birthday parties and Hallowe'en, the very lactose-
crammed orgies sending him to the operating room,

driven there by his parents, two guilty fuckers who
want nothing more than to erase their son's words,

his worry that everyone sounds so far away now.

BLUE PONTIAC

For a few years, every
time my father left for

work, I ran up the stairs
to my bedroom,

lifted the wooden sash
and waved at him as

he backed out onto the
street and drove away,

until one morning
I stopped, bored,

no longer convinced
anything I did would

ensure his safe arrival
at the office or alter

his opinion of me,
a little disappointed

in myself for giving up,
no word yet for apathy,

just the suspicion
that nothing mattered,

certainly not a boy,
his hand fluttering in

supplication or blessing,
nor the father driving off,

unsure exactly what
he was to make of it,

if anything at all.

FORGETTING TO REMEMBER

I forgot again
        to lock the car
                neglected to press
the handy fob
        two times
                as instructed by
the dealer
        the way I forget
                a lot of things
these days
        lights left on
                gloves in pockets
pens, cupboard
        doors agape
                none of which
is as serious
        as cars
                unlocked
an oversight
        I might get
                away with
a few times
        because thieves
                grow old too
forget to
        make their
                neighbourhood rounds
to stop by
        my driveway
                as they have before
to lift the
        driver-side handle
                test my resolve

to be vigilant
     which as I
          have mentioned
I wasn't
     last night
          the result of which
negligence
     was the loss
          of all my change
my glove box
     rifled, its
          contents
spread across
     the passenger seat
          along with the thief's
empty coffee cup
     the remains of
          his brief snack
and strangely
     some leaves
          and other garbage
from his pockets
     presumably
          or hers
though I can't
     believe a woman
          would make
such a mess
     so steeped am I
          in stereotypes
just happy
     whoever it was
          left my glasses
where
     I could
          find them.

OBSERVATIONS

They rub their midnight hands
and in the cold
take turns to spy
on the moons of Jupiter
slaves to gravity
like everything else.

Like everything else
slaves to gravity
on the moons of Jupiter
take turns to spy
and in the cold
they rub their midnight hands.

GATHERING

The vultures rise from the brush
in twos and threes to sulk on branches

of nearby firs and maples every time
I come around hoping to catch a glimpse

of what has lured them to this dense
patch of forest, choked by salal and

junk willow, but their feast lies just out
of sight, hidden in the undergrowth

where I will not venture for fear
it is a cougar's latest kill he may

return to while I am gawking, a kid
caught between curiosity and caution,

unwilling to wait months for a sketch
of scattered bones and too afraid to

risk joining them forever, paralyzed,
able only to exact a kid's revenge by

disturbing these huddled raptors at
their busy work, the dismantling of

some creature, by watching them take
reluctant flight at my arrival, their small

heads twisting to stare at me with what
I can understand only as resentment,

even though I know I'm the one who
is resentful, called away from stoking

the stove, keeping the cold at bay,
drawn by the rush of their great wings.

METAPHYSICS ON THE CHEAP

"On a summer morning / I sat down / on a hillside /
to think about God"
—Mary Oliver

It doesn't take much,
a car that won't start, keys lost,
a faulty stove, no gas in the line.

Inconvenience at most, that's all,
though heaven knows
the newspapers offer more

compelling food for such thoughts,
places my imagination refuses to go,
and which I certainly won't mention

here,
not for the sake of a poem.
Sufficient to say the urge

to dissect is always lurking
somewhere, behind
the cork pulled from a bottle,

the door that closes on
the appalling snow just outside,
questions no more precise

than *why*
most of the time:
Why so short a lease?

Why the expiry date?
The ordinary despair of a
complacent cow

in the chute, curious,
a little anxious, no rebel, hoping only
it will be a lot like sleep.

MATINS

To rise in darkness
for coffee and toast,

in darkness again to
baptize yourself under

the bathroom spigot,
to scrape away the

night's persistent hair,
to select another tie, a

shirt, some socks, on
rare days to sit and

follow a thought until
it ducks under a hedge

and disappears, or
pick up a magazine

and put it down again,
because you're without your

glasses, which are not
glass but plastic and are

on the piano or in the
junk drawer or finally

lost this time for good
and, thus, nothing to fret

about, more reason to stare
through the black kitchen

window at a street distorted
by the imperfections of a

pane that has let in light
for over a hundred years,

to remember the axe
you left head down

in a bucket of brown
water, the chant and

response of the bullfrog's
bagpipe wheeze, the rounds

of Douglas fir stacked five
rows deep in the woodshed.

ABSOLUTION

Of my father
I remember little now
except his meanness
and then only in dreams,
tawdry little scenes
which I repeat

act out—something
in the kitchen,
my own ineptitude,
for which I blame others –
mean myself now

to the point
that what I would say
to make amends
is irrelevant,
the way all apologies are,

so much like the grass we mow
again and again,
or the chair we pick up
and move, unable to place it right,

a promise as distant
as the moon walk,
some fiction on television.

Pettiness is a black coat
we slip on and take off
at will.

If we ever speak the truth,
it is in the small cruelties
we inflict on each other,
how irredeemable
we really are.

SURCEASE
—for Sidney

The water drew her, some said,
using words like moth and flame,

magnet, siren song, but it wasn't
the water, only what it promised

that pulled her from her bed
that morning in the hospital

and led her to the wealthy suburb
by the sea, to the shoreline park

set aside by a developer, a place
originally used to assemble cattle

headed for slaughter, a quiet stretch
for joggers and dog walkers, who

might have mistaken her for another
health fanatic when she slipped

off her clothes and walked across
a pebbled beach into light waves

that offered no resistance to her
determined stroke, to this fierce

and quiet swimmer merging with
a current that carried her south

toward America, her head visible
a while, a witness said, and then not.

FOUR ERASURES

1

Our forest road
after a strong wind,
tire tracks hidden under
needles and leaves,
whole branches.

2

Percy, when they found him,
coffee finished, a glass of
sweet wine barely touched.
In the ashtray a single
plain-end stubbed out,
hands folded in his lap.

3

A carpenter's note
sealed in a glass jar, tucked
deep between two joists,
the paper's edges moth-eaten,
a working man's careful script
recording the cost of lumber and
nails on May 17th, 195_,

4

The neat hole
a groundskeeper excavated
under my father's grave,
the weight of my mother's ashes
as I knelt
to slip them inside.

FROM THE LAND OF SKY-BLUE WATERS

My father made a kindling stick
from cedar he pared back with his hunting knife
to form a broom of sorts that blazed
with just a spark,
a neat trick I learned along with whistles
fashioned from shoots of alder,
how to grease a pair of boots
and take the measure of a tree's height
without leaving the ground.
White-man's wood craft,
Ernest Thompson Seton called it
in his book *Two Little Savages*,
which I read again and again
before there was such a thing as irony,
unaware of the title's racist slight,
happy in the dying years of the fifties
to string a bow, let loose a rough arrow,
its tip a shard of stone I'd split and bound
to the shaft with string.
Kla-how-ya, I said to my grandfather
each time I greeted him,
and vowed to call my house *Wake siah* too,
journey's end, a name I wouldn't understand
for years, that I'd been on one
all this time, like my father
and my grandfather,
who called a thing *skookum*
when it was strong,
mesachie when it was bad,
words that were useful, once,
in the flow of commerce, the sale of
salt and furs, ceremonial
capes and hats.

FERN ISLAND CANDLE®

Match to wick, then flame, a resurrection, courtesy Value Village.
For only eight dollars my friend lives again in this paraffin shrine

fashioned from sand and driftwood and wax and maidenhair
fern, which I picked up and put down, then purchased only because

he had made it forty years earlier—or not, busy man that he was,
supplying craft fairs, boutiques, the Hudson's Bay, a businessman

with hired help who combed beaches for him, the forests,
set the moulds, trimmed waste, so for all I know he may never

have even seen this refugee from the landfill. In our bathroom
it casts a familiar antique yellow, its trademark glow, comfortable

as the 70s soft rock of its time, the marketable light we had
almost forgotten, as we had almost forgotten him, his drowning.

It took four decades for someone to say *enough is enough*, to
relegate their dated kitsch to the thrift store shelf to sit among

beer mugs, Tupperware, toaster ovens and fondue pots, where
this relic will return when I am done with it, done with nostalgia,

the search for time lost, friends who have disappeared, happy
for now to let it burn and brighten, brighten and burn, to revive

those days when the metaphor of the candle, what it means
to snuff out, to be snuffed out, was still a metaphor.

GARY

Lived under a tree
for two years.

Took a bullet in his leg
running from his brother.

Had a nose for water,
an ear for nighthawks, a
taste for wild mushrooms.

Made poultices from
willow bark.

Hated small talk.

Praised the mycelial mat
and the healing powers of tea tree oil.

Rolled his own
and drank a pint of Appleton rum
every Friday.

Disappeared during his last days,
some said into the bush, others,
onto a boat.

Dealt with death
the same way he wrestled
reluctant bolts
from engine blocks.

Like the time
he stood for hours to
film a hummingbird
on its nest and

stayed up all night
to keep the raccoons
at bay.

WEATHER NEWS

New Year's Eve, 1929,
my mother, her boyfriend,
dance at Saint Mary's Hall.

"Festoons of evergreen
lend a seasonal touch and
Japanese lanterns hanging
from steel girders flicker off
and on. Two hundred
revellers welcome 1930
with much gaiety and mirth,"

or so reads an account
in next day's newspaper.

His name was Ivan,
dead now, my mother too.
A few weeks into January,
Ivan's father blows out
his brains, leaves a mess
for his son to find.

No snow that New Year's,
driest on record.
Summer comes, Ivan heads
for England. My mother marries
a decade later, dances again
at St. Mary's. His name
was Ron. Also dead.
No walk in the park,
that man.

Out the window, clouds,
a darkening sky.
I'll be shovelling soon.
More tomorrow, so they say.

PRANAYAMA

PRANAYAMA

A cough persists. A
cut refuses
to heal.
A road dwindles to
a path and then
to nothing.
Day darkens. Night's
moon goes on
vacation. A bird
strikes up a
conversation with
itself. Tides
roll back over mud.
Clouds hang
lower and lower.

It rains.

Small fish abide in
rocky pools. An
alley fills with
echo. Stars puncture
the slate wall of
dark. Newspaper
catches light under
cedar kindling.
Hay fields, then a house,
appear through forest.
Skin knits a
cryptic scar.
Sleep gives way
to waking, eyes
still closed.

ON AGING

Children are all about their new teeth,
outposts of hair, pencil marks ascending

the door jamb, the numerical advance
of grades, height, years, their growing

importance and prestige, life for them
a series of doors opening upon more

doors, a stroll along time's midway where
seasoned hawkers pitch their wares of

ice cream, rock and roll, coitus, defined
benefits, passports, *satchitananda*, a

summer cottage, until someone finally
dims the lights as they do in Joyce's

"Araby" and the stalls close one by one,
leaving only grubby men arguing over

pounds and pence while shop girls flirt with
the enemy, the curtain of illusion instantly

so thin and sere even the most oblivious
can see a world where those-who-can

buy sailboats, tickets to Morocco, happy
to take up painting, register for workshops

in ceramics, while those-who-can't worry
about lack of dental care and extended

health, the cost of a new roof if they have
one, their bones settling, skin turning to

desert, conversations sounding more and
more like the lyrics of popular songs written

years ago by the young who had no idea
what they were talking about, none at all.

SHELF LIFE

Our car lasted twenty years.
Bread stays fresh for a day.
The Bible defines an average life span as three score and ten, four
      score if one is strong. (It also says most of those years are filled
      with labour and sorrow. Living longer is no blessing and nothing
      to boast about.)
Shakespeare hasn't worn out his welcome yet.
Stars continue to astonish, prime numbers too.
Vinyl is proving resilient.
Sex abides among the young.
Single malt Scotch never gets tired.
Spring and summer always receive good press. Fall, not so much.
Nothing beats a decent hurricane.
Elvis is done.
Serial killers dominate police procedurals.
Who doesn't love a perfect mandarin orange?
Christmas, however, disappoints without fail, a perennial kick in the
      teeth.
Cigarettes have had their day.
Swimming naked at night is a dependable joy.
Pet stores proliferate.
Old men buy boats with sad predictability.
War endures.

THE RITES OF SPRING

Lawn thatchers, house painters,
sod aerators, gutter cleaners,
fence menders, window washers,
tree pruners, rat catchers, yard
waste removers, junk dealers,
Roto-Rooters, chimney sweepers,

hoofing it door to door, going
toe to toe with smug retirees,
teenage layabouts, stay-at-home
dads, housewives, girlfriends,
boyfriends, live-in maids and
nannies, renters, do-it-yourself
homeowners,

talking tough about biomass,
invasive plants, water shoots,
post-hole rot, moss damage,
sun damage, frost damage,
salt damage, wind damage, fog
damage, tree roots, creosote
buildup, relentless wear and
tear, the ravages of time, use
and abuse, entropy, seismology,
recent shifts in magnetic north,
climate change, gamma rays,
ultraviolet radiation, bird shit,

offering special deals on TSP,
TLC, psi, elbow grease, one-time
seasonal sales on paint, tar, shingles,
drain tiles, fertilizer, lime, gravel,
grout, lumber, insecticides, pesticides,
fungicides, reduced rates for seniors,
heart-stopping two-for-one giveaways,
money-back guarantees, certified service,
licensed operators, Better Business
Bureau ratings, WCB approval, free
estimates, family-owned quality,
community integrity, pure serendipity

because we currently have people
in your neighbourhood all week
for a limited time in teams of three,
working alone, dawn till dinner, on
weekends and holidays, ready to
serve your every need if you just

set up an appointment, sign
here, give us your phone number,
your email, your next of kin, a
chance to prove ourselves, the key
to your back door, a post-dated
cheque, your full attention, a
break, for Christ's sake, a glimmer
of hope, a future for our kids,
a good reason to say no, to refuse
this opportunity of a lifetime,
to look us in the eye and tell us

you're busy, your dog just died,
you already have someone,
you'd like another quote, some
time to read our brochure, our
hasty note, our handwritten ad
because you're not sure, still on
the fence, on a pension, just out of
hospital, selling in a few weeks, re-
thinking the whole idea of property,
new to this area, reluctant to commit
even though anyone can see

your place is a disaster, its curb
appeal is zero, neighbours hate you,
you've reached a tipping point,
your equity has never been lower,
a stitch in time is not rocket science,
you're cutting off your nose to spite
your face, you're only fooling yourself,
you're a coward at heart, it's about
class, not money, your days are
numbered, this isn't over.

THE THINGS THEY'VE RUINED

The blackberry pie we thought
safe in the warming-oven, the

cobs of corn double-bagged on
the counter, multiple heads of

garlic. The jar of honey one fell into
and was subsequently buried in

beside the woodshed five decades
ago. Bar after bar of soap on the wash-

stand next to the outdoor shower. The
mango some guest left in the fruit bowl

because it was a fruit bowl and the mango
a fruit. Bags of oatmeal and much sugar

in the clay pot. Rolls of toilet paper and
on one occasion even the telephone line.

For some reason a box of Brillo steel wool
pads under the sink. Hours of sleep while

nocturnal hordes trooped through tunnels
of insulation in walls, floors and ceilings.

Our ethics each time we set a lethal trap,
and then our lust for blood when we traded

spring-loaded death for a jail cell. Summer
mornings when we transported these captives

like 18th century criminals to distant forest
realms from which the possibility of return

was unlikely and where we released them
into tangled vines of Himalayan blackberry

so there would be seeds for them to eat,
hoping but not knowing for certain they liked

seeds and thus would thrive, persuaded by
our own pastoral yearnings they would be

thankful, if they could be thankful, to return
to a simpler world, a conviction that weakened

on stormy evenings with each cry of a
predatory owl, each drop of rain that fell.

And, ultimately, our sense of entitlement,
our place on the ladder, yea, the very ladder

itself, when, once, sitting very quietly on chairs
in the middle of the kitchen, we watched

a pair of them slide down the drain mat into
the sink, climb back up and do it again.

VOLUNTEERS

A wild plum behind
the garden shed
throws off buckets of
small gold fruit,
radiates
self-sacrifice,
nobility, compassion.

My father once praised
a scruffy runt
of a zucchini
that had sprung up
in his compost pile
when I was ten.

We commend people
who dole out
bread and soup at
shelters, go from
door to door for
cancer, diabetes, MS,
raise their hands,
offer to stay behind,
step out of lifeboats
so that others
may live.

In streets and
empty lots, in
swamps and marine
estuaries, armies of
seeds and spores
parachute daily
onto sand, debris,
garbage, salt marsh,
bare cement.

Rhubarb, blackberry,
along broken and
junk-strewn alleys.

Apple, quince, pear,
beside railway
lines.

Arugula, kale,
raspberry, in gaps
between backyards.

Thousands
of garlic scapes
on rocky bluffs all
over Minorca alone.

Even these small plums,
resolute hangers-on,
globular, pendulous, ready
to fall into hand, mouth,
anywhere.

YOUNGER THAN THAT NOW

The child has done her best. She has done all she could.
She has taken the man up mountains and brought him

safely down. She has taught him self-defence. She has
shown him how to eat properly. She has extolled the

miracle of wind power, the purity of sailboats. She has ex-
plained Foucault and Derrida and Žižek. She has tried to

reveal the mysteries of dogs. She has modelled discipline
when discipline was the last thing that interested her,

and she has even written to him about the endless joys
of surfing. She has presented thrift as a virtue. She has

instructed the man in fashion and music and literature.
She has introduced him to ethical consumer products. In

short she has done everything within her power to bring
the man out of darkness and into the light, and yet the

man remains stubbornly medieval in his habits and his
thought. Not a day goes by when the child doesn't find

the man napping on the sofa or scanning the pages of one
of his ludicrous detective novels. On more than one occa-

sion she has caught him with a cigarette. Against all com-
mon sense, the man will choose his car over his bicycle

to travel a mere five or six blocks for groceries. He leaves
lights on and keeps his house at 22 degrees. He persists in

using white sugar for his tea and he drinks too much wine.
Under the man's kitchen sink are enough bleach and dish

detergent to poison all the oceans of the planet. The man
owns a leaf blower. It seems there is no depth to which

the man will not sink, no lengths to which he will not go
to satisfy an urge, and the child is unable any longer to

bite her tongue. The man may have made his bed, but
he cannot be allowed to lie in it. His bed is everyone's

bed, the child's bed too. Patience pursued too far
becomes a sin, and the child feels her guilt growing

like a cancer she must cut out. Old man, she will say,
the writing is on the wall, but you refuse to read it.

Your rope has an end and you have reached it. Where
is the song that will finally move you? How big a wind

will it take to shake you? What spell will wake you from
your sleep? Watch closely, old man, for I am casting it now.

ON FIRST VIEWING THE EXTENT
OF THE BEAVER INVASION

Shore-bound fir, pine and cedar die a slow
death, roots submerged, a ring of standing

corpses, sad grey perimeter, our intake buoy
also underwater between surface and bottom,

suspended in amber like a prehistoric bug.
Heads glide along, v-shaped wakes trailing,

no longer the millions they once were, their
handiwork visible then from space, retiary

ponds and canals we used to imagine on
Mars, thinking Martians industrious too,

geoforming a planet to suit their needs,
like these voracious vegetarians, mono-

gamous good parents, whose dens we were
taught in grade school are predator-proof.

Atop our Heintzman piano sat a rosewood
box, where my father kept bits and bobs,

including two front teeth of an adult male,
curved and hollow, tips like chisels, lethal

incisors he said would continue to grow
in a circle if the animal stopped chewing

until they penetrated the skull and killed it,
the memory of his words enough to temper

all thoughts of vengeance and bid me pause,
add a few feet of rope to our drowned float,

accommodate these interlopers and their
colonial urge, cut myself and them some slack.

STAT HOLIDAY

February's deep well
blazes with sun this afternoon,
luring shut-ins and lovers
out onto bare winter streets to
walk arm in arm under
naked boulevard trees,
their heliotropic hearts bending
toward light like flowers.

It is Family Day,
and hairdressers all over town
have shut their doors
in its honour. Looking good
will have to wait
'til Tuesday.

The neighbour's mother
has written her daughter
to say she doesn't
believe in obligatory state-
sanctioned expressions
of love.
Biology is no reason
to rejoice.

A good day
for thick bean soup,
a glass of beer,
time to sit and watch these
late rays slanting
through venetian blinds
while Hubert Laws spins,
and everyone waits
for spring's minions to make
their next move.

THE UNCERTAINTY PRINCIPLE
—with apologies to Werner Heisenberg

At the beach
you move a stone
the size of a football and
the world beneath it panics,
runs in all directions.
You want to apologize
for the intrusion,
consider returning the boulder to its place,
the damage that might do,
pause instead to watch
crabs scuttling,
other creatures that bring to mind
a word from high school science,
annelids, you think, and more words,
radial symmetry,
then the briefest glimpse of a classroom,
some girl you sat across from,
who recorded observations
in her small neat hand,
history now,
like your intention
to become a marine biologist,
all those days of sandwiches in wax paper,
an apple or an orange,
the kinds of things that disappear
the very second you expose them
to the light.

TRAVELOGUE

Oh, Marco Polo,
how you bore me
in your Chinese submarine.
You are taking the easy path now
under the world's dark seas,
your hull full of spices and
pine-scented souvenirs.
Will you surface
to climb a palm tree in the Pacific,
snatch a coconut for your breakfast?
When your engine breaks down,
will you grab a wrench
and fix it the way you fixed your
ailing horses?
All the dull details of commerce,
your petty world of trade
and travel—don't you ever
get tired of it?
Wouldn't you rather be in India,
in the high mountains near Rishikesh
to hear the headwaters of the Ganges
as they begin their long journey
home?

THE PARTY

They were told the party was on.
They were told everyone would be at the party.

They should come. They should really come.

But they were of two minds.

It's a party, they said in one mind.
It's a party, they said in the other mind.

Both statements were equally true.

It was a question of timing.
It was a question of distance.

But it was neither of those things.

Do we go to parties, they asked themselves.
Do we like parties, they asked themselves.

Now they were getting somewhere.

(They had been to parties.
There were pictures.)

Parties are like Christmas, she said.
I know exactly what you mean, he said.

She went on to tell him why parties were like Christmas.
He listened politely, saying only, I know, I know, and thinking

parties are like sand,
parties are like water on level ground
parties are like the wind beneath a door.

When she was finished, she asked,
Aren't we done with parties?

What do you mean by done, he asked.
You know what I mean, she said.

True, he did. But he didn't like the idea
of being done with anything.

What's the point, she asked.
Does there have to be a point, he asked.

I knew you were going to say that, she said.
It's a celebration, he said.

All parties are a celebration, she said.
I knew you were going to say that, he said.

The celebration isn't important, she said.
It's the excuse.

The excuse for what, he asked.
Parties are for getting laid, she said.

Getting laid is like sand, he said.
Getting laid is like water on level ground, she said.
Getting laid is like the wind beneath a door, he said.

Getting laid is like Christmas, they agreed.

In the end they chose not to think about the party.
In the end he came upon her washing her hair.
In the end she interrupted him shaving.

In the end they had a good time.
In the end they left early.
In the end they drifted home.

AGAINST AWE

"All wonder is the effect of novelty upon ignorance"
—Samuel Johnson

Star-addled yobs! Pie-smacked,
pigeon-brained, slack-jawed and gaping . . .
at what?

The dawn?
Another night sky?
The undulant sea?

You are leaving your front doors unlocked.
You are setting yourselves up like a house of cards.
You are stepping into the ring without a trainer.

This is no school picnic.
You can't swim in these waters without a wetsuit.

Whatever you are chewing right now, spit it out.
Stand away from the fire.
Put the gun back in its holster.

The first time for anything is always a mistake.
Think of the regret!

The hospitals are overflowing.
It's impossible to find decent help.
The GDP is down.

Soon we'll all be lying in the snow,
our arms at our sides like nutcrackers.
Everyone will want to glitter and swim
with the goldfish.

It's not enough to stand and gawk.
There's work to be done.
What you need is a little history.
What you need is some perspective.
It's time for Hobbes.
It's time for Gibbons.

Bowled over?
Blown away?
Get serious.

EPILOGUE

EPILOGUE

WHAT WE KEEP

The beat,
the faith,
the home fires burning.

The people down,
the good work up,
the undesirables out,
the grass off,
the straight and narrow to,
all of it under wraps.

The books,
the peace,
the house,
the goal,
certain fish,
bad company,
our heads
when all about us
are losing theirs.

The change, we say,
generous over nothing.

Promises, sometimes, and
secrets even when they no longer matter.

Our opinions to ourselves.

Time, if we understand music,
quiet, if we don't.

Our children safe,
our hands off the money,
our friends close, etc.,
a little something on the side.

An eye out for strangers,
a copy for our files,
our shirt on and
our big mouth shut.

Fit, if we can,
our fingers crossed.

Our cards to our chest,
a straight face
when it all goes sideways.

Our cool,
our lips sealed,
an open mind
and our nose
to the grindstone.

The ball rolling,
the wolf from the door,
our powder dry.

WHAT WE SAVE FOR LAST

The maraschino cherry, the olive,
dessert, always,
the work we can't bear, but sometimes
the work we love.
Our apologies, until the moment
they are meaningless,
as well as confessions
to our dying parents,
who offer theirs in return.
Thinning the carrots
because it's just too tedious,
and joy because we don't
deserve it. No gain without pain,
so pain first
without exception,
as in all those years of school and work
until we say enough is enough,
give us our treat, our brief
respite
before what we've saved ourselves
from thinking about
astonishes us,
the way children do
when they hide in plain sight,
crying surprise, surprise.

WHAT REMAINS

The last raspberries
hang weakly now,
like tired children
on the monkey bars
at our local park,
unwilling to admit
night is coming on.

A few have dropped
to the ground,
red punctuation marks
among the last green
words of grass.

I will pick a small bowl,
take it in and place it
on the blue counter
for my wife to find and
scatter across her cereal,
blood offering
from a dead summer.

What remains
comes to us like animals
looking for a place
to lie down,
like feathers fallen
from a passing bird.
What remains haunts us,

a panhandler's empty hat,
driftwood,
shards of pottery
in a garbage pit.
What remains sings to us
when we are not listening,
writes us letters
that get lost in the mail.
What remains is what we
cannot remember losing.

ACKNOWLEDGEMENTS

Versions of the poems in this collection have appeared in the following places: *Bookends Review, Cede Poetry, Delmarva Review, Event Magazine, Firewords, Framing the Garden* (anthology), *Juniper, The Malahat Review, The Menteur, The New Quarterly, Poems on the Abstracts of Carle Hessay* (anthology), *Prairie Fire, Refugium: Poems for the Pacific* (anthology), *River River*, SAND, *Stag Hill Literary Journal, Sustenance* (anthology), *Times Colonist.*

The quoted line on page 52 is from "Everybody Knows" by Leonard Cohen, from the album *I'm Your Man* (Columbia Records, 1988). The quotation at the top of page 64 is taken from "Song of the Builders" by Mary Oliver, from *Why I Wake Early* (Beacon Press, 2004).

I would also like to acknowledge both the Canada Council for the Arts and the BC Arts Council for their support over the many years it took to write and assemble this book.

In addition, I would like to thank my writing group, The Sunroom Poets—John Barton, Kate Braid, David Eso, Wendy Donawa, Jim Roberts, Kayla Czaga, Kyeren Regehr and Jenny Boychuk—for their help in making many of these poems better.

Finally, I wish to make it perfectly clear that without the inspiration, love and encouragement of Patricia, this book would never have seen the light of day.

ABOUT THE AUTHOR

TERENCE YOUNG recently retired from teaching English and creative writing at St. Michaels University School. He is the author of several books: *The Island in Winter*, shortlisted for the Governor General's Literary Award for poetry and the Gerald Lampert Award; *Rhymes With Useless*, a runner-up for the Danuta Gleed award for short fiction; *After Goodlake's*, a novel and winner of the City of Victoria Butler Book Prize; *Moving Day*, nominated for the Dorothy Livesay Poetry Prize and the City of Victoria Butler Book Prize; and *The End of the Ice Age*, a collection of short fiction. Young lives in Victoria, BC.